A Book of Prayers for All Your Cares

Written by
Michaelene Mundy

Illustrated by
R. W. Alley

ONE
CARING
PLACE

Abbey Press
St. Meinrad, IN 47577

To my mother,
Dorothy Feagans O'Neal,
who was a wonderful example and
taught me to talk to God.

Text © 2004 Michaelene Mundy
Illustrations © 2004 St. Meinrad Archabbey
Published by One Caring Place
Abbey Press
St. Meinrad, Indiana 47577

Library of Congress Catalog Number
2003116165

ISBN 978-0-87029-382-5

Printed in the United States of America

A Message to Parents, Teachers, and Other Caring Adults

If you picked up this book for a child, you already know how prayer can get us through some tough times and comfort us. You want children to find solace as you have.

The hardest thing in writing this book was to write "generic" prayers—instead of "specific" prayers which are more my style, and perhaps more the style of children. And so I hope you will consider this a book of prayer *starters*. Let the children fill in the specifics. Mainly, this book is intended to show children that God is approachable and we can all talk to God in our own words.

Yes, traditional prayers are important, too, even though they are not included in this work. Let your own family and community traditions lead the way.

Speaking of "leading the way," it is so important for us grown-ups to "model" praying. To truly believe that prayer can be helpful, children need to see and hear people in their lives turning to prayer. I remember as a child being very upset when my grandfather died. I asked God to send me a sign that Granddad was happy and okay in heaven. Being a child, I requested a bicycle as a sign! My mother later shared that, when she looked in on me that night, I had fallen asleep with a smile on my face. I don't know if I ever told my parents about this prayer, but on my birthday, one month later, I received a red bicycle—not a new one, but a reconditioned one. It didn't matter; God had given me a sign and I didn't worry about Granddad anymore.

I hope this book helps you to share God, to share yourself, with a child. In sharing your faith you will be blessed with seeing the pure, innocent faith of a child, and you will both walk away being strengthened in your faith life.

God bless you and the young ones this book will be shared with.

—*Michaelene Mundy*

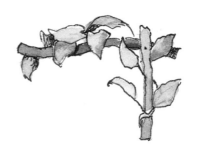

I'm Feeling Angry

Dear God, I know you love me and want me to feel good and calm—not mad. But I am so mad right now. I don't like the way it makes me feel. I want to yell or cry or throw something.

Please, God, help me not hit or hurt anybody while I am mad. Help me to understand I can still make good choices even when I am angry.

I Don't Like Being Sad

I feel so sad today. I want to cry. I feel bad all over and even my head and stomach hurt. Help me to understand what makes me feel sad and to remember the good things that have happened today. Help me find something to do that will make me not feel so sad.

Help me to talk to someone about how I feel. I know I will feel better if I don't let my sadness be a secret.

Help, I'm Scared

Dear God, I feel so scared. I don't like the way being scared makes me feel. I feel alone. I know you are my friend and you love me, but I need someone I can see now to help me.

Mom and Dad always tell me there is nothing to be afraid of. But I am not big like them. Help me to be brave, and until then please be here with me.

The Sadness of Someone Dying

Dear God, my Grandma died. I miss her hugging me. I feel so sad. Mom and Dad are sad, too. Grandma was always so nice to everybody I don't understand why she had to die.

Is Grandma with you? Is she happy? Can I talk to her like I can you? Grandma, I miss you. I remember the happy times we had together. You made me happy. I'll love you forever.

Wanting Something

My birthday is coming soon. I love to get presents. I hope I get lots. I especially hope I get this one special thing. Can you whisper into Mom and Dad's ears that they should get it? I don't mean to be greedy, but I really want it.

If I don't get it, help me understand there must have been a good reason. Maybe I can do extra jobs around the house to earn money and pay for it myself? But it would be so nice to be surprised. Thank you.

I'm Lonely and Bored

I feel so lonely today. Everybody is busy. I don't know what to do. I am so bored. I wish I had something to do. Can you play with me? We could do a puzzle. We could color a picture. We could take a walk. I will talk to you while we do it.

Thanks. I don't feel lonely anymore. I have something to do!

Thank You, God, for the Big, Wide World!

Our family took a walk today. We saw lots of your gifts to the world—trees, green grass, flowers, a pretty blue sky with fluffy clouds, and lots of people. People driving cars, riding bikes, mowing grass.

I just thought—people are your gifts to us, too! And those people make things like houses and cars and computers that we can live in and use. You have a great world! I like it!

POINT
LOOKOUT
←

Family Fighting

Mom and Dad were yelling at each other last night. I don't like it. I hide my head under the covers, but I still hear. Dad says he loves me and Mom. They just disagree sometimes.

Please help them disagree more quietly. Please help them agree more. Whisper in their ears while they are sleeping. Maybe they will listen. Good night, God, and thank you.

Feeling Disappointed

I am so disappointed and that makes me sad and mad. I thought I was going to get to do something special today, but Mom says she is too busy and Dad has work to do, too.

I was looking forward to our special day and now it won't happen.

I guess you get disappointed sometimes, too—especially when I don't do what I should. Do you feel mad and sad, too, then? Please help me not to mope around and make Mom and Dad feel even worse that we can't do something special. They did say we will go another time.

Help Me Learn

I don't understand what the teacher is teaching us. I feel stupid because I have to learn so many new things every day.

Sometimes I feel like my friends are all smarter than me. Help me to learn. Help me to listen to the teacher. Help me to ask for help from the teacher or from friends. I know I have learned lots of things before, and that even when I make mistakes, I can learn from the mistakes.

I want to learn this now. Give me your special help because I know that you are a Teacher, too!

We Are Moving, God

We are moving to a new house in a different town. I don't want to go. I like it here. I like my house, my room, my friends, my school. Mom says I will make new friends and have a new room. We will take all of my toys and things. I know I have to go.

Help me not to be scared at my new school. Help me find a friend quick. Please don't let my old friends forget me. Dad says I can call and they can come and visit me, but it won't be the same.

For a while you will be my only friend who is in my new house. I'm glad at least YOU are always with me, even when we move! Thanks.

It's No Fun Being Sick

Dear God, I don't feel good enough today to even want to play. Please help me feel better soon. Stay close to me during my sickness and let me know you always care for me.

If I need to go to the doctor, please make the doctor really smart so she knows what is wrong. And if I have to take medicine or get a shot or stay in bed, make me strong and brave. Give me happy thoughts so that I can heal.

Forgive Me, God!

I lied today. And I didn't get caught, so I didn't get into trouble. I should be happy, but I'm not. I feel bad. I wish I hadn't lied. I don't like feeling this way.

Help me tell the truth even if I get punished. Help me not to chicken out.

I'm feeling better knowing I will tell the truth even if I get sent to my room with no TV tonight.

Give Me, Patience, Please!

I want everything in a hurry, God. You probably noticed. I want my homework done right away. I want the car ride to my friend's house to be quicker. I even want to grow up really soon.

I also want big people to pay attention to me when I say something. I don't like it when they just say, "Oh, that's nice, now run along." Please give me patience to be a kid. It takes a lot!

Michaelene Mundy is the author of three other books in the Elf-help Books for Kids series. A school guidance counselor, she has also taught elementary school and has worked with learning-disabled children. She holds master's degrees in school and communty counseling, as well as in education. She is the mother of three children.

R. W. Alley is the illustrator for the popular Abbey Press adult series of Elf-help books, as well as an illustrator and writer of children's books. He lives in Barrington, Rhode Island, with his wife, daughter, and son. See a wide variety of his works at: www.rwalley.com